Footfalls

Footfalls

Poems of the Camino

Suzanne Doerge

SHANTI ARTS PUBLISHING
BRUNSWICK, MAINE

Footfalls
Poems of the Camino

Published by Shanti Arts Publishing
Interior and cover design by Shanti Arts Designs

Cover image by Joe Gunn and used with his permission.
Interior images [page; creator; year; source; license]:
[2] CarlosVdeHabsburg, 2019. Wikimedia Commons (CC BY-SA 4.0)
[10] Juanje 2712, 2010. WC (CC BY-SA 4.0) [13] 083794703875938,
2012. WC Public Domain [15] 083794703875938, 2012. WC PD
[16] Loreto Carmona, 2013. WC (CC BY-SA 4.0) [26] José Antonio Gil
Martínez, 2005. WC (CC BY-SA 2.0) [32] José Antonio Gil Martínez,
2008. WC (CC BY-SA 2.0) [38] Xurde Morán. WC (CC BY-SA 2.0)
[47] Simon Burchell, 2018. WC (CC BY-SA 4.0) [52] Niederkasseler,
2012. WC (CC BY-SA 3.0) [54] David Roulston. Used with his permission.
[58] Eduardo Miyake, 2021. WC (CC BY-SA 4.0) [66] Niederkasseler,
2011. WC (CC BY-SA 3.0) [75] Hibiscus7, 2020. WC (CC BY-SA 4.0)
[81] Víctor Pascual Ruiz-Ogarrio. PD [88] Lala Lugo. WC (CC BY-SA 4.0) [92] Delmi, 2007. WC (CC BY-SA 4.0) [98] José Antonio Gil
Martínez, 2004. WC (CC BY-SA 2.0) [102] Javier Casado Tirado, 2009.
WC (CC BY-SA 3.0) [108] Lameiro, 2017. WC (CC BY-SA 4.0)

Shanti Arts LLC
193 Hillside Road
Brunswick, Maine 04011
shantiarts.com

Printed in the United States of America

ISBN: 978-1-956056-39-6 (softcover)

Library of Congress Control Number: 2022942998

To the footfalls of all pilgrims in all walks of life

CONTENTS

FOREWORD

For over a thousand years, people have walked the Camino (The Way of Saint James), an ancient pilgrimage that leads to Santiago de Compostela in northwest Spain. Even when setting out alone, a pilgrim is accompanied by many. Listening closely, a *caminante* absorbs the footfalls of millions of pilgrims over the centuries.

At a time when many have put aside traditional religion, we find ourselves seeking a direction or deeper meaning in life. It is this quest that propels many to walk the Camino. Whether inspired by what Jesus meant when he said, "I am The Way," or by another source, amidst the comradery and routine of walk-rest-eat-sleep, on the way to Santiago, you come across the shared teachings of many traditions—contemplation, compassion, community.

Bringing only a few belongings, while carrying the weight of a lifetime, pilgrims ponder what to leave behind and what to take up in the rest of their lives.

I traveled the Camino in 2016 with Joe, my life companion, or *compañero* as we call ourselves from our years in Nicaragua during the Sandinista Revolution of the 1980s. We walked for a month on the Camino Francés through four autonomous regions (Navarre, Rioja, Castille y León, Galicia). As we stirred up memories of lands across the ocean colonized by Spain, we rediscovered some of the ruthless sides of history while listening for liberation inspirations within Christianity.

It was Joe who had the insight that when traveling the Camino, there are three epiphanies each day. The first—WONDER— when you begin before daybreak, sweeping the flashlight to find waymarks, your footfalls uncertain, wondering if you have lost your way while being swept up in the wonder of wandering under the stars and into the dawn.

The second—DELIGHT—takes place just as de(the)-light begins to infuse the sky. You stop for a pastry and cappuccino, then rejoin the path that is now exuberant with textures and colors. Your walk fills with awe and gratitude for Mother Earth. Your footfalls invigorated. Yet this is followed by the inevitable third epiphany—EFFORT—when the sun is high, your aches are piercing and your feet "fall" on the path. Exhausted, you may doubt if you can reach that day's destination.

It is the deepening cycle of WONDER, DELIGHT, and EFFORT that informs the titles of three poems and is reflected throughout this collection.

A pilgrim may sense the footfalls of a lost loved one, an ancestor, or spiritual guide traveling with them. For me, it was my friend Beth, a painter of landscapes and the sacred, who died of cancer three years previous. Her sense of wonder and delight lifted my footfalls and whispered the pines.

My effort was heightened by having developed plantar fasciitis in training for the Camino. Like many who are injured, I had to swallow my pride, stop, and search out a ride to catch up with my traveling partner. However, it was this "fall" that gifted me with time to chronicle how light sojourned the landscape, taking up residence in my pace and in the footfalls of people I met along the Way.

This collection of poetry is a harvesting of that light.

Shadow Pilgrim

She first appeared in early morning
much taller than I, her thin legs
extended out before me,
pilgrim of the Middle Ages.
Dressed in pants, like a man, as if
from my time, perhaps for her protection.
She walked in my shadow, even though
I had set out to walk in hers—
our hats, bundles, steps lifting-falling in sync.

I asked her why it was she walked the Camino.
Her only reply was the ceaseless click of a wise, old
walking stick and the slosh of water in a gourd.

In silence, we walked on, bound to one another.
With each step I took, she stepped too—
over roman bridges, across cobblestone roads,
through abandoned villages.
I pointed to the ruins of the 10th century pilgrim hostel
just as she raised her hand to do the same
as though to say, she had stayed there once.

When I slogged to climb the slope, she slowed.
When I sat to catch my breath, she plopped down
at my side; her pack at rest alongside mine.
Slurping merciful water from the village fountain,
we both bowed our heads in gratitude.

As morning passed, without a word, she grew shorter,
just my size, walking softly by my side.
Where I turned my gaze, she gaped there too,
breathing waves of wheat and vineyards of promise.
Both of us nodding with the sunlit sunflowers
that brightened our stride.

Sometime past noon, she flagged behind,
her feet still tied to mine;
as I turned to tip my hat, she tipped hers too,
as though to concede it was my turn to take the lead.

Late afternoon, she finally spoke in a whisper
of shuffling leaves—
"What has the Camino taught you so far?"
I pondered, walking a few more hills and valleys.
Finally, I replied—
                We are never really alone.

NAVARRE

The Camino, she said,
peering into my eyes
as though I could comprehend,
will be a condensed experience
of your entire life

Traversing the summit
into churning wind
persistent pilgrims trudge
heads bent, thin.
Alto de Perdón—
we are forgiven

shifting shadows in the olive grove
medieval monastery ruins
still at prayer

Roman cobbled roads—
built by forced labor
stone by stone;
backroads for Franco's troops—
no wonder
so much pain
under foot

¡Escucha! Listen!

Swinging her walking sticks
click .. click .. click .. click

una peregrina viene
a pilgrim is coming

down the paved street at daybreak
dup .. dup .. dup .. dup

across the wooden bridge
PLUNK .. PLUNK .. PLUNK .. PLUNK

along the uneven roman road
clabble .. caclabble .. clabebel .. clabble.

la peregrina se va
the pilgrim moves on

to the dirt path beyond
thud .. thud .. thud .. thud

a leaf drops
phlun

WONDER

Early risers labyrinth through dimly lit streets
past houses with their eyes shuttered closed
into the wonder of dreaming slopes.
Fields snuggle under patchwork quilts of sunflowers
and wheat, while mountains kneel in prayer
beside their beds.

Stars open wide their generous arms
as dazed walkers wonder which way to go,
sweeping their flashlight beams in search
of a *concha* or yellow arrow
painted on a wall, the road, a rock,
looming in a field or cryptic
turn in the path.

Colorless tai chi forms shuffle their feet,
approach and leave, soft breeze—*Buen Camino*.
Behind them, a string of beams wavers across the ridge,
reminiscent of miners just released
from an overnight shift.

Clouds brim with youthful luminance—
pink with a shyness that beckons
eloping hills to emerge from reticent shadows.
Olive trees and clusters of grapes unveil their shapes.

A steeple surprises the horizon; distant mirage
approaches. Fasting wanderers ease into this village,
deep asleep, shutters still closed for more shut eye.
Wondering . . . except for one windowed glimmer
where awaits *café y pan—desayuno de peregrinos*.
Morning has arrived.

Whoosh!

Having reached the summit, strangers gather
for one collective catching of breath.
In silent chorus, our eyes amble
the cathedral expanse, inhaling
nature's blue dome to only then rest
on the stone cross, standing human-size
                    before us.

Shuffling our feet, one by one
our poles discretely lean in
to read the centuries-washed inscription
then sway back, mute, stunned
by a presence
                    we dare not touch.

Each stranger watches the other, speculating
whether anyone else feels the same
on this perplexing pilgrimage—
                    religious quest in a secular world.

Might there be other closet Christians
in our midst? Or someone who left
the church but still is moved
by the prophetic message of their roots?
Too timid, given the sins of the church
to show devotion before the rest of us?

                    Whoosh!
A gazelle leaps up the slope,
catching sight of the sacred in her flight,
the long-legged youth sprints
through the crowd of besieged bystanders,
places her hand firmly on the cross,
kneels and bows to the divine in all.

Choosing a Municipal Albergue

For a cheaper price, he gets a richer experience.
Sixty beds in one room, bunks line up
in numbers, reminiscent of the time
he spent on that navy ship.
Towels and socks hang to dry from rails,
possessions tucked around and under dangling heels.
Just-bathed walkers settle in for afternoon naps
as young lovers touch fingertips across the rows.

Soft footfalls and attempts at silence blend
with murmurs in Japanese, Spanish, Danish, Italian;
English of the Irish, Australians and Scots;
French, German, Korean and, of course,
the universal language—snores.

Grimacing appendages prop up on pillows, the walls.
Everyone coddles cracked and blistered feet, smearing
the latest proclaimed miracle cream.
Stinky hiking shoes exiled outside the door;
one hundred and twenty throbbing feet ease
into the empathetic relief of sandals and clogs.

Cell phones line up to charge at the sockets
while pilgrims slump in their bunks, flipping pages
of the Brierley guide to comprehend where they've been
and fathom the yet-faceless quest on the next day's map.

Pictures and messages sent in fruitless attempt
to convey to loved ones faraway: the rise at daybreak,
the five-hour sojourn to be justly rewarded
with this rest, in the richly textured silence
of sixty wayfarers, sharing one room.

CIRCLE OF LIGHT

Clouded-over dawn
in these shrouded woods,
you flounder off
then on
the path
without a flashlight.

Not knowing your name
nor you mine,
I offer you
this small circle of luminosity;
our steps within its limits.

Shoulder to shoulder
we face uncertain turns,
forward inching in the luster
of our conjoined stride.

Until boundaries dissolve
and all is alight.

DELIGHT

Now that I have left this life,
my paintbrush at rest beneath my easel—
to help you be awake
as you walk the landscape of northern Spain—
        I bequeath to you my sight.

Eyes of a painter, trained and inspired
so that you too will see—
                    shades of color
shifting tones
        textures   and   depth
shadows   and   shapes.

Awake! Don't miss it!
Newborn radiance rediscovers abandoned crevices,
entices the horizon to strum love songs upon
the sky, invites the thinnest of stems to be
at prayer with the universe.

Boundaries dissolve   we are one.

Don't worry, my friend of pen
                    paused in air.

if you can't find the words—that palate
of infinite hues for describing what you see—
        simply let the sights seep
                    deep

and from there, trust—
a syllable will come sweeping
toward you   like that bird of the wild
        just flown from the brush.

As you walk into these days   behold
        and hold   all that astounds.
I bequeath to you my eyes.

THE WAY

If I come across Jesus on the Camino
today, will I recognize him?
Doesn't he say—"I am the Way?"
That passing pilgrim just might be
Jesus on the Road to Emmaus.

The young German seems to have seen him.
She says she cries most nights, overcome
by the compassion of the Camino.
Could he be the Brazilian healer who shares
his cream to soothe my screaming feet?

Or the man with MS bearing his cross
on this taunting path?
Or the Danish couple, who, upon reaching
the rise, scan the vast valley to declare—
"Let's walk this one for the healing of the planet."

Or the companion of my life wearing his Rights
for Refugees t-shirt?
Or the youth who leads me through the serpentine
village, to find him, after two days of separation?

Or the Basque painting a protest slogan
on the wall we just passed?
Or three stranded, ailing pilgrims—
Italian, Honduran and Japanese—
who console each other cooking a meal
and taste him in their midst?

Will I recognize Jesus on the Way?
And if I do, will I be able
to take up his pace?

CONFIANZA

It's all about trust,
the young Costa Rican exclaims,
over the morning's *café y chocolatine:*
I've gone through life
building walls around myself
afraid to risk, step out on my own.
Sin confianza.

Until here, on the Camino,
at last! I dare
to travel alone. No one knows
who I am, where I'm from
what I've done.
Free to become whoever I want.

But then, I got injured. Terrified
outside my walls. Certain, I couldn't
go further. The whole trip, over;
I would return home a failure.
Who did I think I was?

Only to find, to my surprise,
there were angels who would catch me—
a hostel host who said I could stay a few days,
a massage therapist who appeared in the night,
pilgrims, like you, who held me as I cried.
Angels who gave me the courage to say:
"It'll be okay. I can go at my own pace."

And to trust, *confiar*, for the rest of my life—
there will be angels ready to catch me
as I catch them,
and when there are not, *con confianza*
I will catch myself.

SILENT SENTINELS

It is in the twilight
between waning moon and daybreak
fearing
you may have lost your way
that the sky begins
to cantor silhouettes—
blackened stems of steadfast weeds
silent sentinels
clusters of attentive friends
lined up along your route.

IMPRESSIONS

Over twelve hundred years of pilgrim
        soles thumping this terrain,
the landscape and our feet—
        both made of clay
wobbling on the potter's wheel—
        mold one into the other.
Glazed with memory, fired with change.

Rolling meadows slide into
        slopes at the base of our toes.
Boulders snuggle up to hillsides as
        heels round to the back of boots.

Rows of vineyards march
        the upsurge of our arches.
Hills struggle to reach their summit
        as muscles strain to meet the slope.

Rocky roads—erosion and ruts
        erupt in blisters and punishing sores.
Thirsty creek beds, baked, predict
        brittle fissures that chisel the skin.

Trees reach for the beckoning sky
        as propped up feet, toes to ceiling, relief.
Earth, ploughed at season's end, sighs
        feet massaged at day's end.

Our footprints hollow the landscape;
the landscape hallows our feet.

Soft Glow

Rural Nicaragua, 1986

I lie on a cot in the darkened room
gazing out where she stands
at the outdoor sink
under a tree, loosening
her long thick braid.
One single bulb dangles from a wire, inciting
a halo around her as she slides her hands
under streaming water to splash
the day's dust from her face.

Whispering, so as not to disturb the others
staying in this hostel, a young man steps from
the surrounding night, places his hand on her shoulder
in the way that lovers do in the everyday.
She turns, immersed in his kiss.

>   Tenderness in the night.
>   Glow of soft light.

I lay alone just outside the glow, never imagining
that in the dawn, they would part
and his truck, carrying mothers home from a peace
walk on the Honduran border, would hit a land mine
ending their lives and his.

>   Horror in times of war.
>   Blast of screaming light.

In the years that I remained in Nicaragua,
my new-found love would wake just before dawn,
leave our bed, my loosened braid.

>   Glow of soft light.
>   Tenderness in our sight.

Traveling to the Honduran border to visit projects
in the countryside, he too could meet danger—
war zones, long uncertain drives home.
Always, the precarious kiss goodbye
in the way that lovers learn to do,
everywhere, in times of war.

Northern Spain, 2016

My love of 30 years slides down
from the upper bunk in the haze of first light
while I lie in the lower one, stay behind,
rest my leg. I will catch up, take a bus.
I imbibe his every move as he gathers up
his belongings to venture into the countryside.

>Glow of soft light.
>Tenderness in our sight.

Whispering, so as not to disturb the others
staying in this hostel.
"Do you have enough food and water?
Today's a long walk between villages."

>I close my eyes.
>Abiding kiss goodbye.

No war here, all is safe. And yet,
a tremor echoes through some dimly-lit
passage, deep inside.

COUPLES ON THE CAMINO

For those of us who choose
a life together—couples on the *camino*—
the landscape is a map of all we've traversed
unfolding as we draw nearer—

      steep climbs, sweet descents
paths discovered or never found
      rapids laughing our canyons
despair of late-summer creeks run-dry
      dark caverns we dare not enter
supreme satisfaction of hay bales stacked.

In the course of this long walk, sometimes
side by side, in silence or in conversation,
we become one in the landscape of our lives—
      paired shadow of unspoken rhythm.

Other times, each of us at our own pace,
dip solo into fluting ravines, pick
baskets of berries (maybe for sharing),
ask the path to bring us together again.

We are the view from the mountain's ridge—
where we have been, where we will be—
only glimpsed from where we stand.
Propelled by determination, time and again

two pilgrims on a promenade, we stumble
our way through twilight's fog into
the warmth of day, casting changing shadows
as sun rays blaze our silhouettes.

TOURISTS AND PILGRIMS

Tourists and pilgrims
What's the diff' anyway?

Both take photos
to show where they've been.

Both stand on street corners with
puzzled faces, maps in hand.

Both squint eyes to study coins
holding up the check out line.

Both keep local economies afloat
at the risk of drowning the local.

Both have been coming here
for hundreds of years.

Tourists and pilgrims
have much in common,
even if we like to think
ourselves distinct.

Except

one comes to see the sights;
the other walks inside them.

RIOJA

Remove your hiking shoes
you are standing
on holy ground

I don't know
why there is so much fuss
about snoring in the dorm;
when I wake up
everything is perfectly hushed

Irresolute morning mountain
bright-eyed on one side
shut eye on the other

The Camino always
keeps its promise
to take you
to the next village ....

....
....
.... eventually

SHAKE OFF THE STORM

2016

Three of us ramble out of town
into persistent night; beams of our flashlights
sweep the meadows. All other pilgrims,
forewarned on this stormy morn,
snuggle in their albergue beds.

Lightning flashes! Floodlight splashes
raven-tinctured fields.

The guidebook reads:
"These low-lying meadows were notorious
for witches' covens." We shudder.

Ominous piles of rocks point the way
into a scraggly forest. We freeze.

1656

We sneak out of town
under the shelter of darkness, our long skirts
sweep the meadows.
      Guardians of the commons
caretakers of the herbs
            moon dancers of the tides
     ushers of birth
our feet tread softly on sacred Earth.

We assemble outside church authority, just beyond
the reach of the priest, our husbands, our fathers.

There are those who seek
             to enclose the commons
bottle our healing power
                     claim it for their own
        license it, sell it
                     put us on trial
as they will do in Logroño, just a few hours
walk down the road.

2016

Shaking off the storm, we follow
the benevolent banquet of centuries-old stones
into the enchanted forest.

It's a good thing they didn't burn all of us.

PILGRIM ROUTINE

Like walking with Ghandi
on the 24-day Salt March,
or Padre Miguel D'Escoto
on a 14-day Stations of the Cross

for peace in Nicaragua,
or Cree youth on a 1600-kilometer
trek for Indigenous rights
from Whapmagoostui to Ottawa

or like monks in a hermitage
or nuns in a cloister—
each day greets us with discipline
of deepening routine:

rise to the first glint of day,
pull on same clothes,
gather up belongings—
caminar, caminar, caminar

move at meditation's pace:
climb, rest, descend
exert, rest, reflect—
caminar, caminar, caminar

arrive at the abbey, the convent,
an encampment, a benevolent village:
to wash, wring and hang the day's clothes,
rest, coddle feet, eat, drink, sleep

another daybreak, wake
begin, all over again—
caminar, caminar, caminar
our souls imperceptibly altered.

THE GAZE

Iglesia de San Pedro de Viana
—*for Valentina*

Youthful solo traveler
sits on the old stone wall

of the bombed-out church;
dome opened to the heavens.

Her dreams release like doves
into crimson sky

for all she has lived
and all she will become.

My seasoned eyes
trace her gaze

into the expansive valley
that stretches out before us

to where it slopes up
into limitless indigo ridges.

I look back,
she is gone.

She has places to go.

Packing Instructions

Pack two pairs of socks
one for your feet
the other for your hands
for those cold mornings
when you ask yourself—

*What was I thinking
not packing gloves?*

We Shall Not Cease from Exploration
—after T. S. Elliot

Exhausted, we reach
each day's port of relax after
10-20-30 km of forward rowing.

Among us, couples ignite or rekindle love,
mothers and daughters bridge generations,
fathers and sons deepen their bonds.

Young and old venture a solo quest
to know themselves, their bodies,
the sacred, the world.

Each of us trundling our own ponderings
as we mumble *Buen Camino*. I stare
into the candle, you left lit in the chapel.

I too reach the rise just beyond what,
anticipating a response in the expanse
below, the drawing in of breath.

In the end, we discover the answer
was with us all along, dozing
in the alcove where we began.

Walking the Vineyards

Imprisoned in maroon balloons
tethered to bridled vines
                    a lifetime
lined up in countless rows   languishing
like an overdressed high school band
in a stalled, mid-day summer parade.

It would be an act of charity after all,
just once   emancipate
one cluster   or two   or four
burst free your sweet wet
between my desert teeth
                              release
your exquisite temptation.

I offer a much better destination
than smashed   trapped in a bottle
slapped with a label   shipped
to some far-away table   to make
an unknown someone famous.

Forgive me Jesus, I may be about to sin.

My hand on the fence,
I glance up and down the path
to see   if anyone will notice.

CAMINOS

Se encuentra con personas de todos lados.
On the Camino, you meet up with people
from everywhere, they say.

Except   if truth be told   rarely
from the poorest countries of the world.
(You may meet only one or two
from Central America, Africa or the Caribbean)
When we do, they are likely
to be clearing our table or mopping the floors
                              after we've moved on.

Why would a child who already walks
        12 kilometers to town with a few pesos
to buy onions and salt,
        or a refugee family who fled to the border,
or an old man who crosses the city daily
        to tend someone else's garden?

They walk their own Camino
                              every day.

COMPANION TRAVELERS

We wake before the break of day, here
and around the world, in the company of many.

We rise from our bunks, hammocks,
and pallets on the floor amidst whispers
and rustling of belongings.
We pull on yesterday's clothes,
stumble into tired shoes or plastic sandals,
splash our faces, brush our hair,
crave *café y pan* somewhere en route.

With a wish of *Buen Camino*
we lift our packs, baskets, and buckets.
Refugees hoist bundles hoping to reach the border;
women balance artisanal wares on their heads;
men bend their backs to lug harvest to market;
youth slug up slopes to plant tree-prayers for the planet.

We step on the path, leap into truck beds,
and squeeze into overcrowded buses; chug
down dusty roads and darkened paths. Our hands grip
walking polls, leather reins, children's hands.

We begin the ascent, keeping pace
with the reluctant break of day.

Click of sticks, spin of tires, slip of hoofs—
to the next village, bustling market, abating river,
churning factory, fecund field, menacing border.
Some of us will face a sudden heart attack, bullet or
landmine. Continue on or end it here.

Histories and languages interweave as
we recount our stories in soft voices.

Roosters crow, church bells ring, dreams lift
along the roman-cobbled road, the highway, the trail—
past fences, creek beds, and military check points
into the radiance of the pregnant countryside
giving birth before our eyes.

We journey in the company of many
to feed our hearts, our families.
heal the world, the Earth.

ADVANCED PILGRIMS

We are the *advanced* pilgrims, the ones
who meet up at bus stations and beside
fliers of locals offering rides.
Feet propped up on our packs
walking polls collapsed.

Quick to tell our woes:
                an old sprain
a pulled tendon
        a troubled knee.

We assure each other—rest
an absolute necessity.

We must travel the Camino, each
at our own pace, we say, sipping
café con lèche in some quaint café.

Even in Medieval times, injured pilgrims
must have had to accept a ride.

Besides, we have a job to do.
We advance ahead of our traveling friends,
secure a bed for their day's end,
get a taste of the best place to eat.

We, the *advance* team, will never
cower as we wheel into town.

"*Con permiso* Señor, drop me off
  one block before the albergue, *por favor.*"

ORCHESTRAL

Instruments settle in, nestled in bunks
counting on a whole rest or at least a half
night's sleep, until the curtain parts
and discordant tuning begins—

first in that corner, a trombone inhales,
then in this corner, a French horn blares.
Oh dear God, hear that groan
next to me, a saxophone.

Wand lifts. Let the symphony commence—
garbling and snarling, gasp and release.
Blanketed bugles, pillowed percussions
tuned to the rustling of sheets.

Until .. shhhh, can you believe?
the symphony finally reaches its finale.
We, who must perform tomorrow's
morning serenade, roll over in relief.

At last, sleep....

That's when... Don't tell me!
The cacophony rejuvenates.
Clarinet below the exit sign, cello by the door,
flute by the washroom, kettledrum at my feet.

The conductor, again, has fallen asleep!

DIPPING INTO THE COMMONS

Inhaling our bottle's last drops,
we trudge into the next village.
Shutters shut tight to the scorching sun,
only one lonely dog to greet us.

We would feel forgotten, if not
for the *fuente común*—
ancient grace of liquid and stone,
tree and bench, quiet and shade—

refreshing steadfast oasis.

A village tradition of traveler's respite
offered up by invisible hands—
invoking time-honored splashes
of children laughing in creeks
and women chatting at wells—

we dip into the commons.

Water, freely given, like the river
that once flowed pure.
Giggling springs before
they were silenced,
given a bar code and tossed
in high risings of waste.

Fuente común—gush of mercy
in these times of prolonged droughts
when women walk further for water
and corn shrivels in the fields.

We cup our hands
to catch the crystal miracle,
rinse our dusty faces
baptize away the sins we walk in.

We are reborn, village after village
in this stream of silver
compassion *del fuente común.*

We bow our heads
fill our bottles.

TIMELESS DESIRE

Our arms swing with those of countless
peregrinos who trekked along this shaded river
in long skirts and cloaks, on foot, on horse,
clutching water gourd, wood staff or sword.

They slept under this tree, or its branched
ancestor that sowed a seed for future ones.
They curled up for the night down by this creek
or blessed a bed in that relic of a pilgrim hostel.

Ready to sacrifice everything, even
their lives to make the journey.
Their wounds tended by dedicated religious;
their lives protected by the Knights Templar.

Keeping their promises for petitions fulfilled,
believing in the power of divine will
to end harm, cure ill, usher in goodwill.

With each swing of our arms, we flow as one
stream into the timeless desire
of humanity to make itself whole.

SEEDS ON THE WIND

There are those who die on the Camino
causing us to pause before crosses
                    bearing names
cobbled cairns of wood   photo   stone.

Foreboding messengers
sudden appearance on a ridge, by the path
sends trembles through our ribs.

Pilgrims, unable to keep pace with
aspirations, unprepared or unrealistic,
halted by weaknesses in our bodies
                    we are yet to face—

heart attack or stroke on a rising slope,
unexpected distance   heat   dehydration
or cut down by a car as we come to
naively believe pilgrims own the roads.

Each is drawn to something beyond their reach
                    ancient and worthy.
They arrive   they disappear
                    flap of a map   notebook   pen.

Seeds on the wind   swept away,
whole lifetimes borne on the breeze,
                    certain to land in some quiet
furrow of embracing earth.

If you had to die unexpectantly, could there be
                    a better way?

SOLE TO SOLE

Hiking shoes drenched in pungent aromas
snuggle up to one another.
Banned from the dorm, as rumors of
their stench migrated here long before
them. Bought for comfort, soaked
in sweat, dumped in dung, forced
to conform to the unique stride
of the *caminante* who wears them.

Haggard hiking shoes (unable
to keep pace) forsaken
       along the way.
Flung in ditches and creeks, dangling
from trees and telephone wires
       or worse—
plunked on a rock pile, calvary
of someone's pain. But then,
there are the distinguished ones,
proudly placed on display, adorning
the portals of fine-dining restaurants.

All of them, unattached. Out all night!
       Imagine
how they fool around when
no one is looking!

As for the boots and shoes who made it
to this *albergue* shelf,
each one heaves a sigh of relief.
Long standing pairs celebrate
as they know what it takes
to stay together this far.

Set free from the feet that dictate
their every move, compliant shoes
        loosen up
                let their tongues flap
                      get in touch
with each other's soles.

No matter the country they are from
or how exploited the labor behind
the label, while *peregrinos* sleep
jubilant shoes open wide their eyelets
        let down their laces
                tap their heels and
                      tip-toe revolt
delighted to have another night off.

PENSIÓN FOR A NIGHT

You trace the contours
of my hills and valleys
then step back
on the Camino
to walk them

SOMEONE WALKING BEHIND

What about those times
when walking alone
you're certain you hear
someone walking behind?

Shuffled footsteps, thud of a pole,
slosh of a pack against the back
but when you turn around
there's no one there.

Startled, at first
you take a second look
then settle in
as you begin to comprehend

whoever they are—
a pilgrim of the past
an ancestor reaching out
an old friend not letting go

Jesus, Muhammad or Buddha
strolling the Earth again—
it is love
that accompanies you.

Untitled

be

can

one   there

than this   oh yes

hill

no higher

can be

there

ANOTHER WAY

"Con permiso, Señor. ¿Donde puedo tomar el bus a Nájera?"
"Excuse me sir. Where can I catch the bus to Nájera?"

"Al otro lado del pueblo," he points casually, up
    the taunting incline into the village, perched
    like a cobblestone hat on the top of a giant's head.

I gape as wheels spin, hoofs stumble, knees strain
    to approach the church at the summit.

"Up there?" I cringe, trying to catch his eye again.
"Then down? The other side?" My injured foot
    wails with dread of the inevitable decline.

"Si Señora," he nods, turning to get on with filling
    his truck. My foot flinches, resists.

Another local approaches from a threshold
    where he must have been listening in:
"Señora, there's another way. Simply go down
    this road and circle round the base of the hill.
    You'll find the highway on the other side."

Smiling at my relief, his well wishes
    lift my feet—

"Todo en la vida tiene solución,
    solo para la muerte no hay remedio."

"Everything in life has a solution,
    only in death there is no remedy."

All that Glistens

I want to join the line for communion,
heartened by the compassion of this priest,
his blessing of the pilgrims
his offer of a place to sleep as albergues are full—
                    just like an inn keeper
                    2000 years ago!
His homily praises women through the ages
standing strong at the base of their crosses—
                    just maybe there is
                    a place for women!
He invites us sojourners, as he lifts the host,
to love one another along the Way.

But my attention slowly ascends
from the marble floor of this 600-year-old church—
                    I'm doing the math,
                    flipping the history pages
                    watching ships come in
up the lustrous altar that stretches to the towering ceiling.
                    Gold, all Gold.
Mary, Joseph, and the twelve, draped in gilt
from head to foot.
                    I mull it over at the jewelry counter—
I can't hear the invitation to communion anymore.
                    His invitation, drowned out
by the cries of the Inca, Maya, Aztec, Aymara

Then, as today—
                    mining the heart of the sacred—

beating drums of Zimbabwe, Ghana, and Mali.
Tears cascade down this altar.
Welded to my pew, I am
unable to join you.

RAINY COLD AFTERNOON

Across the ridges, translucent ponchos flap
billowing deceit, porous foes purchased
for two euros in case of days like this. Soggy
lifeboats cling to drowning *caminantes*

but I am even more chagrined, as cold streams
trespass the brand name label that so earnestly
promised resistance (store clerk's insistence,
"Oh yes ma'am, it's guaranteed").

The flood that Noah was told would never
come again is storming the sealed seams
to submerge my *quick-dry* clothes.

Somewhere. Anywhere.
Some place dry.

Cow bell rings, we're in this together—
sad eyes, puddles and mud,
hunched backs and skid of hoofs,
mine as sodden as yours.
Bereft, we turn our heads, in search
of someone, anyone, who will let us in.

Blurred horizon, faded in the wash—
all gone gray: the road, the sky, our hearts—
distances further than ever imagined.

Somewhere. Anywhere.
Some place dry.

Surely that far away
blur is the
cheerful village praised in the guide.

CASTILLE Y LEÓN

on the way to Santiago,
the rising sun
always has your back

                             ancient and modern
                               side by side
                              time stands still

¿Quieres bailar?
Cumbia, Merengue, Salsa
mocked the poster

                           yesterday's wash still damp
                               she climbs the hill
                                  steaming

Bus Pilgrims

We were timid, at first, embarrassed in fact.
Quick to give excuses, the few of us huddled
waiting for a bus. But after one week on the Camino,
I fear there won't be enough seats for all of us—

eager to board with our packs and pains.
Enough of twists and relentless strains!
On board, we collapse like walking poles
each in our own compassionate seat.

After days of our feet pounding the Earth's
heartbeat, we are estranged.
Perched up high, peering down, we marvel
like museum visitors through giant metal frames
at a living painting of able-bodies moving on.

Picking up speed, the landscape, now blurred,
cradles slow moving pilgrims, strung like
scattered beads on a long-looped rosary
handed down through generations.

The bus arrives, much sooner
than I would hope—
life shrinks when you go fast.
I step down, feet on the ground,
re-enter the oeuvre we are becoming.

Village Sueños

Yawning villages of narrow, cobbled streets,
terracotta tiled roofs and long-serving metal hinges
wheezing open timeworn, wooden doors.

Sleepy villages—brought into being by wars
between kingdoms, perched high on hills for defense,
left stranded, far from the water, long after
anyone remembers what the fighting was for.

Worn out villages—lulled to sleep by large-scale
agribusiness putting to rest family farms;
construction and mining dormant; youth exiled
to cities to shake awake their livelihood.

Abiding villages—kept alert by the endless flow
of wayfarers, each cradling their own dreams.

Vigil(ant) villagers rise to meet traveler's every need:
menu de peregrino—early dinner at 7:00,
fresh baguette with wine, uncorked and poured;
farmacias stocked with braces, foot remedies
and socks; blessings from nuns and priests dedicating
their call to the journey of pilgrim hearts.

Every morning, church bells ring, shower
Buen Camino on each sojourner moving on.
Sheets changed, floors washed, dishes put away.
Food gathered, bread baked, vegetables chopped.

Until the belfry in the afternoon rings the news—
next wave of pilgrims coming through.

Leaving just a slice of time for the people
of the village to live their own *sueños*.

PAUSE

If we hadn't

paused

on our forward
march
to adjust our
packs,
we never would have
                    looked
        back
    to
spy
in sandstone cliffs
ancient hermit caves—
persistent remnants
                    of
                deep
        religious
contemplation.

MEANT FOR YOU

Yoko can't bear to wear her hiking shoes
tormentors of her troubled pace.
"These are meant for you," the store clerk,
in the upscale athletic store, had said.
But these days, she carries the pair in her pack—
luxury boats with holes in the middle of a lake
—meditates on excessive weight.

Seeking relief at a café-bar, she lifts
a cappuccino to her lips and sips
fear: "Slogging along in these sandals, I'll never
reach Santiago."

A stranger collapses in the chair beside her,
leans over: "Do you have a knife?
This boot tortures my bunion. I gotta cut
open the leather. If not, I'll never
make it to Santiago."

Having passed this pilgrim along the Way,
without really seeing her, Yoko looks at her now.
Deciphering the English, with care, she assembles
the words. "Perhaps . . . these were never
really meant for me." She pulls from her pack
(already feeling lighter) her wider, softer hiking shoes.

The sister pilgrim eases her skeptical feet into
them   long sigh   slow smile   moist eyes.
"Then these," she lifts her boots, "are meant for you."
Yoko slithers into them . . . a just right fit!

They would never meet again, but with
520 kilometers to go (and countless ones beyond)
where one stepped, hill or valley, village or field,
there would always step the other.

.

¿Algo Más Señora?

i

If you ran a village restaurant in a house built
400 years ago, with stone-framed windows
welcoming in the sun

under a low ceiling of hand-hewn chestnut beams
clutching a vine that took 16 years
to grow across them

all to the sound of bells ringing from an
800-year-old belfry, next to a roman bridge
that has offered passage for nearly 2000 years

you would never be in a hurry
to make my sandwich.

ii

To the resonance of violins, he solemnly slices
the cheese and ham, devoutly cleans the blade

  hungry *peregrinos* bow their heads
  in the doorway, approach
  the counter on either side of me

he anoints with oil the oven-warm bread
and graces with lettuce, pickles and tomatoes

  I glance over my shoulders to make sure
  the newly arrived know this is my sandwich

he christens with spices planted, nurtured and
harvested from his fecund fields

    on this race to the sacred, *peregrinos* mumble:
    gotta get going to get a bunk for the night

he glides his hand across the counter
to select the perfect knife

    peregrinos shuffle their feet, look at
    their watches, consider their options

he pauses the blade at the preordained angle
and places the sacrament on a plate
just as the concerto reaches its diminuendo.

Having finally forgotten why I would be in a rush,
he looks up, to rest his eyes in mine,

    ?Algo más Señora?

EFFORT

Tears of despair in the night
only halfway to Santiago
just maybe
I can't make it.

Feet on the path in the dawn
already halfway there
just maybe
I can!

BUNK 132

Assigned to Bunk 132
rows of two-tiered boats
lined up in a harbor.
I spread my gear across my allotted deck,
slide my sandals into the hull
and nestle in for another night's voyage.

Sojourning sailors, we slip into a sea of dreams:
emergency exit lights—our stars,
clothes dangling from rails—our sails.
Boats creak as we toss and turn,
propelled by murmurs of mother tongues
blowing in from across the globe.

Just before dawn,
some raring seafarer's foghorn alarms
signaling shore has been sighted.
Land approaches sooner
than the rest of us had hoped.
I roll over—*Oh please, let us drift*
back out to sea.

One by one, beacons stir dark waters.
Shuffle of crews—stuff duffels,
wiggle into shirts and pants, descend ladders.
Shipmates pass in whispers
charting their course, step onto the wharf,
look back to ensure no precious
cargo remains in the hold.

Moorings secure for the next sojourner
we swing our packs over our shoulders
and reclaim our walking poles.
We stroll the shore once more
with hopes to reach at end of day
another stargazed harbor.

BUEN CAMINO

Peregrinos in the city can be easily spotted.

No need to hang a *concha* on their pack,
or wear a pack at all, to distinguish themselves
from tourists and locals.

One simply needs to note the tick in their gait,
the hesitant pace, the worn walking shoes
or when seeking relief: socks with sandals,
flip flops or clogs or nothing at all.

Adorned in the fashion of a long camping trip:
mixed- unmatched, men with scruffy beards,
women with hairy legs. Porting the tell-tale
wrap round the toe, the ankle, the knee.

But even more than all of this, *peregrinos*
never blend in—
after 10 days on the Camino
they've come to believe, in spite of
the urban chill, everyone wishes them good will
as revealed in the subtle smile, glance of the eyes,
nod on the go—
     Buen Camino

Never met before, or only once,
having shared a room or a moment on the road
seeing each other time and again
or never again.
     Buen Camino

No Place to Go

Cold morning in Burgos,
albergue closed, no place to go,
too painful to walk the sites.

Wait for an afternoon bus
with hopes of catching up,
sore legs and feet elevate
across a frigid bench.
I cringe as I attract attention;
curious passersby, each
with intentional stride of those
with a place to go.

My belongings in bundles
beside me, I wrap myself
in my sleeping bag liner.
Surely now they will think
me homeless on the streets.

A real urban *peregrino*,
like ones in cities,
on park benches, same
as this one, all over the world.

SANTIAGO MATAMOROS

Stunned by my first sighting of you—
peaceful pilgrim forced onto a horse
elevated sword slashing the Moors—
I am shame-footed. I am self-condemned
recalling a conversation with three friends—

"I am going to walk the Camino," I had said.

"What's that?" asked the first, her last name Mohamed.

"An ancient pilgrimage in Spain, sort of like walking
 to Mecca," I ventured.

"If so," she kindly smiled having just returned from
 her once-in-a-lifetime Hajj, "once you reach
 your destination, you will be a new person."

"That's what they say, but we will see.
 Actually, it's also an ancient route trenched
 in driving the Moors out," I winced.

"I know about that," stepped in my second friend
 a recent Moroccan immigrant, "those were my people."

"Oh," I replied, my blue eyes looking through the centuries
 into hers of brown. "I suppose I can't avoid the historical
 sin we will be walking in."

"You will be well accompanied," she assured. "Muslims believe,
 after being banned from the Garden for eating the fruit,
 Adam and Eve wandered the earth separately for 200 years
 before reuniting at Mount Arafat, near Mecca."

"I know what it is to take a long walk," leaned in my third friend.
 "We walked for five days during the war in Somalia. We had fled
 but my brother and his family were still in Mogadishu, so we
 returned to get them. I carried my nephew on my back."

"We will sleep in hostels, bunk beds, I am told, and eat pilgrim
 meals along the way. Where did you sleep? What did you eat?"

"Under trees. We carried a small supply of food and water,
 walked by night to hide from planes dropping bombs," she mused.
"Oh, I said," fidgeting the snap on my pocketed pack.

"Today, many make their pilgrimage to Spain in boats, fleeing
 drought, dreamed destination never reached," asserted the first.

"Is it possible," I asked, tilting to hear my Muslim friends,
"when I arrive in Santiago de Compostela, everything
 will be revealed? Having eaten the apple and completed
 the quest, at long last, we all will step
 down from our horses, drop our swords,
 care for our shared garden?"

CROSSING THE MESETA

will do for shade
n
g
i
s
d
a
o
r
a
n
e
v
when crossing the meseta e

poplar leaves applaud
another meseta-scorched pilgrim
makes it to the village

At the base of the cross
in Mansilla de las Mulas
two exhausted pilgrims
set in stone on the steps
weep
for all the suffering
they have witnessed
in the world

WAVES

''We travel the Camino in waves,'' the Swiss muses,
 having sat down with strangers to share a *menú del día*.
"Each wave carries drops from distant seas—
languages, ages, cultures and stories.
We wash up on beaches with the same pilgrims
 at *albergues* and cafés. But as I had to remain
in this town to heal my blister, my wave moved on."

"I get your drift," jests the man from the U.S.,
 passing the jug of wine to his newfound friend. "I was
traveling with five. We met in Pamplona,
each from a different country. We surfed crests
I'll never forget. But after a few days
in the hospital, I lost my wave."

"You know," adds the Australian, passing the basket
of oven-warm bread, "each of these surges
is like highway traffic. We complain of congestion—
too many pilgrims crowding the route—tailgating.
But if you slow down, the traffic rolls
on and you find yourself in a silent trough between
the waves. With no one around, you hear the click
of your own stick."

"True, but you can't deny," smiles the Australian,
 pouring the pilgrim from the States another glass of wine,
"Camino is community *en camino*.
If you pull over onto the shoulder, scoot to a stop
just past solitude, another pilgrim wave
comes rolling through, with its own tidal pull."

''Like all of us meeting here," splashes in the Swiss,
 bumping his chair up against theirs.

SHE OFFERS

I suppose I should not be surprised
    to find her here
        on an early fall evening
            in the profound simplicity

de la Iglesia de San Martin.
    Here, where she has taken up
        residence for a thousand years.
            Her vigorous swim

through Romanesque arches
    stirring awake the mellow stone.
        Here, where she proclaims miracles
            in the soft curves of brick

her agile stretch up, up to
    eternity`s dome where she scoops
        the universe in the depths of me.
            You will meet her

in the side chapel
    shepherding luminosity
        to grace creatures of the mystics
            hefting pillars to the heavens.

She offers to envelop us
    in her exquisite silence
        entices us to dwell
            in our innermost still.

I am certain I have spied her before
    on an evening like this—
        whisper-glistening
            through my kitchen window.

LOSING THINGS

The things we lose along the way:
the pants fallen into a crack
between the bunk and the wall,
essentials tossed in the lost and found—
Would that be my scarf she is wearing?

Water bottle I forgot at the top of the hill,
hat left on the table in the café-bar,
flashlight dropped when I bent to tie my shoes
in the glare of the plaza, unmissed until
the dark edge of town.
No going back.

Reminders of the things
I didn't know I could do without:
clothes in my closet that I never wear,
resentments that no longer matter,
failures that were only glitches,
sorrows that stir into sweetness,
longings that discover presence—
all stones to be left at the Cruz de Hierro.

The finding of ourselves in the losing.
Our packs all the lighter.

THUMBS UP

My name is Ela.
I cross borders.
I hold up my thumb
to say—*Good to go!*
My hair, I wear
the way I choose—

no gender binds me.
I dive into cities across the globe.
I once slept with rattlesnakes in the desert.
I lost my pack. I don't need all that.

I talk to my blisters, say, *Toughen up!*
For my evening rest, I trot
barefoot through gritty streets.
There was a time
when humans had no shoes.
Time is due. Get back to basics.

As I walk the Camino,
I am

gender bending
border bending
rule bending
time bending
and talking with you, right now
we're generation bending.
Hey. What do you say?
Thumbs up!

AT THE LAUNDRY SINK

My love and I meet up
at the outdoor laundry sink
too exhausted to speak.
He, after a 22 km walk
in the relentless heat
of the merciless *meseta*.
I, after a morning of meditation
in the cool still
of a Templar chapel.

Side by side:
I lift a wash basin
onto the shelf
and he lifts one too.
Without a word,
we each draw water
to soak our clothes,
as women around the world do—
in refugee camps and creek beds,
in dirt patios and basements,
alongside rivers and
at the mouth of wells.

In unison, we immerse
our day's dust into
the water to wash clean
our separate revelations.

After rinsing and wringing,
we hang them in the sun.

Urban Pilgrimage

i

day off in León
lost in the crowds
we nearly lose sight of
why we are here

ii

faces of meeting-up pilgrims
glow in the plaza—
stein glass reflections
of León's grand cathedral

iii

everything we forgot to bring
were learning to do without
can be purchased
for a price

iv

white sheets, white duvet
sweet dreams in a soundless cloud
pensión for the night

v

leaving urban jungle behind
songbirds herald new birth
countryside

FIELDS OF WHEAT

We met when our hair was wheat
flowing on the plains of Spain—
waves of gold dancing the fields
earth beneath our feet
burst of promise
trust in harvest
the bread we would bake
piles of hay for jumping in.

But late summer, cancer took my hair
fall then winter, earth laid bare.
Until spring, another chance
plough and sow, sprouts
rose across my sunny slopes
until wheat began to blossom
again, renewed.

I didn't see you then—
soulful friend of my youth—
you were gone, living your own life;
yet always my wheat danced with yours.

Until, cancer returned to sweep away
the yield from my fields again—
fallow and seed, fallow and seed.
Then one day, in early winter,
my ploughed earth went utterly barren.
To dust I returned.

You weep since I've been gone—
without us having had the chance
to dance in the wind again—
our hair, our feet on the earth,
we never got to bring the harvest in.

But now I beseech, as you walk by.
Don't look for me in the newly cut fields;
I am no longer there.
Instead, listen, to the whispering pines
that sway just beside,

here is our dance and our love—
forever green.

SANTA MARÍA

—after prayers to Virgin Mary posted on chapel walls

Santísima Virgen del Rio—
Blessed Virgin of the River—
pools of gentle swirls
cool breeze on shaded path
liquid miracles of tender love.
       Permíteme que os llame
       madre, nombre tan dulcimo
Allow me to call you mother
so sweet a name.

Santa María del Camino—
Blessed Mary of the Way—
beneath your gaze
this flame I light
for all those I love, for all that worries me.
You understand all my joys and sorrows.
I walk with you, in gratitude.

Santisma María —
Most holy Mary—
birthing luster on walls of the Templar Church
softly chanting wisdom through a rose window.
       Me conforta
       y llena de confianza—
You comfort me and fill me with confidence.
Blessed be the fruit of your womb!

Virgen María de la Luz—
Virgin Mary of the Light—
Your moon in the sky through the night
all the day
       me ha salvado
       y hecho feliz
has saved me and made me happy.
You illuminate the path within me.

Virgin Peregrina—
Virgin Pilgrim—
wise companion of the spirit
audacious mother of the son
living temple of the holy trinity.
You completed the difficult Camino of your faith.
as you broke from the crowd to hold
the eyes of your son on his Way
of the Cross. You felt
his suffering and walked
with him.
My mother, my sister through the ages.
May I too know courage and compassion
in all the days of my Camino.

Mientras vivo en este
valle de lágrimas—
as long as I live in this vale of tears—
I walk with you, oh daring *peregrina*
alongside those who are persecuted
for the sharing of loaves and fishes.

Mi esperanza,
mi refugio, mi amor—
My hope, my refuge, my love.

Por los siglos de los siglos
Amen

PRAYER

"I don't want to reach Santiago,"
he confesses, with a hint of Honduran accent.

"My priest suggested I walk the Camino,"
he confides, kicking a clod of dirt.
"He believes it will help me
get perspective, now that I'm settled in the States.
Time to consider what I want of my life, besides
earning money at a job that I don't enjoy to buy
more things I don't really need."

"But I fear when I reach Santiago
nothing will have changed. I'll go home to find
everything exactly the same."

"I'd do fine if I could be on the Camino forever.
Wake up each morning, know where I'm headed
with a plan to get there. Walk all day,
arrive, sleep, get up and do it again. The life!"

Shrugging his shoulders, he saunters a stretch
ahead. Ambling and gazing up into the overcast
sky, his fingers stroll a string of rosary beads:
thumb and fingers at prayer.

As the last invocation sifts through his lips,
the sun slips past a cloud and casts a shimmering
beacon on a towering thistle, brown and dry, beside
him in the field.

This grasps his sight; he halts in his tracks,
I halt too. He looks up,
adjusts his pack and picks up
a quickened pace.

THE CAMINO TEACHES YOU

trust what the day will bring—
    after yesterday's 5-hour trudge
    in crushing sun, too much,
    pack up at dawn, get back on the path.

embrace routine—
    wake up, walk, wash, eat, sleep
    same shirt, same shoes
    boring to accepting.

greet limits—
    swift footsteps passing
    you on the path, satisfied,
    you arrive what some might call
    late, at your own pace.

summon perspective—
    overwhelmed by how far
    you have to go, look back to
    view how far you've come,
    heartened, accept one step at a time.

be compassion—
    hand extended to a stranger, especially
    when you don't know it's needed,
    stirs courage to ascend the next slope.

traipsing through this learning
you intuit along the Way
the landscape, the passing pilgrims and you
have become interlaced.

BETWEEN THE MARGARINE AND JAM

At this breakfast table of sleepy hikers,
coffee and pre-dawn air stir us
awake for the steep climb ahead.
"Et vous?" I ask the elderly gentleman
who arrived late the night before
greeting everyone in French.

*"C'est ma septième promenade
et mon dernier à 87 ans."*
His face luminous, but reticent
as though there's no way to explain
across the vast expanse of language
and bustle of a breakfast table.

As if it might be worth it to try again
between spreading the margarine and the jam,
he draws from under his shirt a painted
wooden cross with three joined hands:
black, white and brown.
"Pour la paix," he nods,
"tellement nécessaire dans notre monde."

No matter the languages we speak
or the countries from which we came
between the margarine and the jam
I nod, he slowly smiles back;
I believe. I understand.

CRUZ DE HIERRO

Lifted up the slope by the singing
of long-robed Benedictine monks,
we begin our hushed ascent—
flexuous ribbon of dawn-trekkers—
to the Camino's highest peak
                    la Cruz de Hierro.

Bent with the weight of stones
we have carried far too long,
pause to catch our breath—
sunrise promise on our backs
casts rose-scarfed sky up ahead.

Pines line the upper path, whispering:
                    I know you can.

Pyramid of burdens laid at the base
of the iron confidant. I ascend.
Stones of those before me
shift beneath my feet, rolling free.
I weep as I fill the newly cleared space
                    with my stone.

Sweet descent, released
down the cairn, down the mountain
wind in my hair, freedom in my heart.
Ave Maria spreads her wings
                    across the ridges.

GALICIA

One day
trudge up heartless mountain:
No more!

Next day
amble down generous slope:
More!

In land of the Celts
it should be no surprise
that grain bins
for the harvest
perched on stone stilts
appear as altars
rising in the mist

dung on the road
too tired to step aside—
my stinky boots
stinky-er

hillside meadow
late summer calls—
stop, lie down and sleep
you have nowhere to go

Gaudi's Inspiration

It must have been
this very woods in Galicia
precisely at this
time of the morning—

        dignified oaks: pillars
        poised to prop up the sky,
        branches raised in silent prayer,
        sprinkled with choirs of brambles and vines,
        consecrated in speckled luminance—

that inspired Gaudi
to build magnificent
cathedrals and palaces,
in his meager attempt
to replicate the divine
that dwells so perfectly here.

La Corredoira

La Corredoira, old sunken road,
emerald tunnel of earth and canopy,
moss and stone—patient messenger
entwining villages and farms—
worn deep by countless water droplets and
pilgrim feet over hundreds of years.

Sweet chestnuts, venerable oaks
adorned in moist ruffles of ivy vines,
line up on either side, facing one another
across the narrow thoroughfare.

Ferns arch their necks, on the lookout
for approaching pilgrims on the path.

A cow bell sounds in the field,
granite rocks commence a beat,
rusty wired fence strums a tune
as breeze and wild brush stir up the verse.
The festivities begin.

Giant oaks lift from the moss
their ponderous roots to crisscross the road
trunk to trunk—do-si-do
tossing back their leaves with abundant glee.
Steadfast banks lean back to watch
as enchanted grasses sway with bliss.

Until . . . ferns stand up straight,
sound the alert: *a pilgrim approaches!*
All freeze, except for a newly sprouted twig
who can't help but giggle.

Old trees heave a sigh of relief;
another pilgrim naively believes, the slight
sway they see is only a passing breeze.

Our Lady of the Mist

It was in
the early morning
of a quiet Galician glen,
amidst the mist, apples and ivy,
after all that she had seen and come to know,
that Mary, mother of Jesus (born without
sin, as all women before her and all
women after) lifted her
long blue skirt
to dance.

STROLLING THE GALICIAN COUNTRYSIDE

i

no work in town
table of crafts
for sale on the path

ii

moist leaf turnips bounce
in wagons behind rolling tractors
promises fulfilled

iii

thinly sliced slate fence—
a lifetime to stack
lifetimes to last

iv

strolling the pasture
swinging my black journal
filled with verse,
like my farming ancestors
swinging their Bibles
on the way to church

v

steep mountain meadow
expansive valley below
arms open wide
invite you
to fly!

IMPRINTS

They are here in these fields
most often spotted in the early morn
when the mist is just like this.
                        Do you see them?

Cautious caretakers of persistent
Celtic beliefs emerge from the underworld
to weave and leave white webs in the grass.
Fairies, flying alongside the path—
their enduring translucent wings—
believing in us, as we pass.

But more often these days, their wings
go limp, burdened by our footprint,
now much wider than the soles of our feet,
much weightier than those of pilgrims
who left their imprints here before us.

Modern-day footprints magnified
by fossil fuels that brought us here;
electricity charging through our homes
even when no one is there,
plastics on our backs
while oceans rise and wildfires blaze.

Shhhhhh . . . listen in the brume.

Wings flutter the air
a wisp of prayer—
                        Lighten your step.

Only then will the wee ones
trust us enough
to let us see them.

LIGHT THROUGH OPEN DOOR

He was only half awake,
meandering through Palas de Rei
just before dawn,
when he passed an open door
of the church he had left behind
year's before—
        soft glow invited him in.

He found himself standing
before a statue of the Virgin Mary,
awakened by unexpected singing
sweet and sacred,
calling up in him
all he had once believed—
        the miracles, the sacrifice,
        the steadfast love—

llamados de ser testigos de amor de dios,

listening presence of the Mother of God.
He gazed into her eyes
as she gazed into his.

He wept
all the tears he had left
from his childhood.

LOVE SONGS

i

It is here
I love my man
sitting on a time-honored stonewall
gazing into the baffling fog
believing in what will be
when it dissolves

ii

Ambling the ghostly countryside
he sings Spanish love songs
anhelo del corazón
lucha del pueblo—
all is possible
on this path
opening hearts
healing our common home

Ancestors Speak

We are here—
past inhabitants of this land—
in the foggy thin spaces
of numinous landscape.

We appear as phantom trees
and floating mountain tops,
breathing horizons of wisdom
long after our crossing over.

Ancient trees seep their lore
deep into descendant roots
as in the land where
your people are from.

Red rivers flow lament
through your veins too—
the taking away, the clearances,
the rapes, the uprisings.

Having called up your ancestors
in these days of the Camino,
they too accompany you
on these last footfalls to Santiago.

SANTIAGO TO THE ENDS OF THE EARTH

Goddesses
line the road—
after a night of rain
swishes of leafy branches
sprinkle down on us
their holy water—
as we pass beneath
their generosity
on these last 20 kilometers
to Santiago

ALWAYS

In the early days of fall,
she hooks a bucket
over her arm, just
like her mother before her,
steps onto the patio
and into the shade of a fertile tree.
She glimpses up into the branches,
sun splashing her seasoned cheeks,
to grasp the ripest pears.
She will place them on a wooden table
by the path to Santiago, with a sign
that reads *Gratis o Donativo*.

One could say it's a religious act,
this Galician custom
of welcoming pilgrims,
one that has always been.

At summer's end,
her beloved tends the border
of the field, just
as his father before him.
He chops the lower sprouted branches
from the trees his great grandfather
planted to shade the pilgrim path.
He is older now, arthritis in his hip,
but the trees continue to sprout
so he goes out,
axe in hand, to tend them
as best he can.
So absorbed in his task,
he fails to notice
that he prunes to the tune
of pilgrims passing,
as they always will.

ON THIS DAY

well practiced click
of walking sticks,
hundreds of years
of swaying packs,
feet advance—
in pain and triumph
swift and hobbling
in wheelchairs and runners
crones and youth
athletes and priests
joyful and tearful
profane and sacred
Medieval and modern
mystery and fact
holding hands, going alone—
to the call of
bagpipes and beliefs.

On this day, we are
droplets riding
one great wave,
like the ones
that surged before
us and the ones
that will roll in after
us, compelled
by an ancient tide
that could never
be held back—
we wash into
the streets of Santiago.

BLESSING ON ALL WALKERS

Sunrise through praying eucalyptus
you are forgiven

A sparrow sings sweet, high in the tree
walk in peace

Mist whispers in the fields
walk softly on the Earth

Bubbles tumble into laughing streams
love all walkers as yourself

Emerald green reveals itself on other side
of the shadowed tunnel
walk toward the improbable
and make it possible

Saint James of the Way

Santiago of Holy Bible and wooden staff,
scallop shell on wide brimmed hat,
peaceful pilgrim of the Way
I saw what they made

of you for their rapacious purposes—
plopped on a charging horse
armed with sword
to slay the Moors.

We bow our heads
to enter your revered place of rest;
what truth can you tell us
of the mysteries of your quest

to the Celtic land of Finisterre
to unearth the good news already here;
dare your ill-fated return to Jerusalem
to consult with Mary, the Blessed One.

What did she say
that you have sought to tell us
all along the Way?

Rolling Away the Stone

They crucified her relationship with Christ,
said she belonged, silent, at the base of the cross
not behind the altar. One among the excluded,
she buried her childhood faith
        deep in a cave.

But these days on the Camino, she has felt
the stone that blocks the opening budge,
having met up with Christ in the actions of others.
Words heard at the village fountain, calling her to act—
        You shall draw living water.

Along the Way, she spied Mary Magdalene,
her curvaceous hair unfurling over her breasts,
anointing with wholeness and unconditional love,
the one he trusted most, Apostle of the apostles—
        Go and tell the others.

Now, in the Cathedral of Santiago, she lights a candle
for all sojourners with whom she has broken bread,
ascends behind the High Altar to hug the jeweled Santiago,
glimpses gems revealed along the Way:
        contemplation, compassion, community.

As she sways with the *botafumeiro* across the sacred space,
she opens the chalice of her heart, pours it out,
walks forward with the others to receive the host.
With all of this, she blesses the sacrament,
        lifts it to her lips.

VILLAGE SQUARE

"Where are you from?" inquires the Irish.
"Canada but originally the U.S.," I reply
 stepping into the village square.
"I have a sister in Toronto," he puts forth,
 his foot patting the worn stone where my foot lifts.
"I'm from Italy but I live in Australia," another pilgrim
 steps in, her hand grazing the lip of the Medieval fountain.
"Really, my mother is Italian, but my father is Greek,"
 he joins us, adjusting his walking stick.

Criss-crossing the early morning village square—
                always there.

You say you don't have the time, the health,
the money to go to Spain, walk the Camino
or return to trek it again.
                No bother, no worry.

In this global world today, we are all
criss-crossing the village square:
in our towns, on city buses, in our living rooms—
                potpourri of humanity.

The opportunities are where we are—
the stranger behind you in the checkout line,
the imported artwork on your mantel,
the traditions of the Indigenous on
                whose land you stand,
the book in your hands—
a tapestry of threads looping over and under
ancestors, cultures, beliefs and languages.

The chance to know ourselves in the daily
criss-crossed encounter with another.

The Camino is everywhere.

TAPESTRY OF LUMINOSITY

Upon leaving Santiago,
each pilgrim, in their own time,
lifts high a sheer silver cloth
until it billows in the clouds
allowing its length to fall soft
across the entire expanse of the Camino.

The porous veil drifts to the ground
where it soaks up the path's many moods,
allowing all pain and disappointments
to sift through.

And as it does, the cloth absorbs
vibrating colors of countless stories told
in hundreds of languages, inspired by
thousands of wisdom words, revealed
in millions of dreams, traversed
by billions of footfalls.

Each pilgrim, in rhythm
with their own heart,
lifts what has become
a luminous tapestry,
draws it into themselves
and offers it up
to those they love
and those they will never know,
with a commitment to walk back
into their life—
emboldened to live it
with authenticity.

THE RETURN

It's not easy, this return
to the busy highway we left behind.
Bones and muscles settle.
Eyes see only as far as our daily lives—
backyards, walls and computer screens.
Ears hear only languages we ourselves speak
as we lay down to sleep.

Feet, tucked under desks like obedient pets
or shackled to gas petals like handcuffs to briefcases,
carry remnants of blisters that chart vanishing
maps of the landscape we journeyed through.
Four regions of Spain hide in our closets
having snuck through customs
on the soles of our shoes.

What has become of the simple routine—
walk, rest, eat, sleep?

We are back to some good things—
a familiar bed, steady roof overhead,
being with the ones we love who know
where we are from.

But as we walk the streets, grocery aisles,
cathedral vestibules, universities and factories,
even the fields and hills just outside of town,
it is our souls that refuse to fully return;
they continue to stroll
with all the souls of the Camino
to Finisterre, the ends of the Earth.

GLOSSARY

Albergue: hostel

¿Algo más señora?: anything more ma'am?

Alto de Perdón: Mount of Forgiveness

Anhelo del corazón: longing of the heart

Botafumeiro: incense burner

Buen camino: expression pilgrims give to one another; literally means "may you travel well"

Café y pan: coffee and bread

Café y chocolatine: coffee and pastry with chocolate

Caminante: walker

Caminar: to walk

Camino: path, road, way, journey

Compañero: companion with a shared commitment to justice; comrade

Concha: scallop shell

Confianza: trust

Confiar: to trust

Con permiso: excuse me

Corredoira: narrow dirt road connecting farms and villages

Cruz de Hierro: highest spot on the Camino Francés with an iron cross where people leave stones, symbols of burdens they want to leave behind

Cumbia, merengue, salsa: Latin American dances

Desayuno de peregrinos: pilgrim breakfast

En camino: on the way

Farmacias: pharmacies

Finisterre: literally "end of the earth"; a rocky peninsula beyond Santiago, once believed to be the edge of the world

Fuente común: village fountain

Gratis o donativo: free or donation

Iglesia: church

Llamados de ser testigos de amor de dios: called to be witnesses to the love of God

Lucha del pueblo: struggle of the people

Menú del dia: menu of the day

Meseta: plains of central Spain stretching from Burgos to Astorga

Pensión: guesthouse

Peregrina: female pilgrim

Peregrino: pilgrim/male pilgrim

Por los siglos de los siglos: forever and ever

¿Quieres bailar?: Do you want to dance?

Santiago Matamoros: St James the Moor Slayer

Se encuentra con personas de todos lados: You meet up with people from everywhere

Sin confianza: without confidence

Sueños: dreams

Acknowledgments

My gratitude—

to Joe, with whom I have the privilege of walking the Camino every day. And who, on this pilgrimage, had to journey with the worry that if I picked up my pen one more time, we would never reach Santiago;

to our son, Benjamin, for his enduring encouragement, and our daughter, Daniela, for her keen poetic insights; both have enriched these poems;

to Beth, for her undying sense of wonder and delight;

to Valentina, an Italian youth who brought us delight as we met up time and again;

to a Scottish couple with whom we shared effort on the journey—David, with his injured ankle, who joined me in taking needed breaks when we would both pick up our pens to write, while his partner, Pam, and Joe, trudged on;

to three injured pilgrims—Japanese, Honduran, and Italian—who made visible the meaning of global compassion in their support of one another;

to my Muslim sisters, who know what it is to walk a pilgrimage;

to Katie Marshall Flaherty, whose skilled editing graced every footfall of this poetry collection; and

to Christine Cote at Shanti Arts Publishing whose deep appreciation of nature, art, and spirit enriches this Camino journey.

"All that Glistens" was previously published by *Peregrine* (Volume XXXIV, 2020).

ABOUT THE AUTHOR

Suzanne Doerge is an adult educator who has worked with organizations at the local, national, and international level to support the voices of marginalized communities. Originally from southern Illinois, she lived in Nicaragua during the 1980s where she met her *compañero*, Joe Gunn. They live in Ottawa, Ontario, Canada, on the unceded land of the Algonquin people, where they raised their twins, Benjamin and Daniela.

As a facilitator in the AWA (Amherst Writers and Artists) method, she guides creative writing workshops. Her poems have been published in several journals and anthologies, in print and online. This is her first poetry collection.

SHANTI ARTS

NATURE ▪ ART ▪ SPIRIT

Please visit us online
to browse our entire book catalog,
including poetry collections and fiction,
books on travel, nature, healing, art,
photography, and more.

Also take a look at our highly regarded art
and literary journal, *Still Point Arts Quarterly*,
which may be downloaded for free.

www.shantiarts.com